Draw Your
PET!

You Can Draw

Exotic Pets!

Katie Dicker

Gareth Stevens
Publishing

Please visit our website, www.garethstevens.com. For a free color catalog of all our high-quality books, call toll free 1-800-542-2595 or fax 1-877-542-2596.

Library of Congress Cataloging-in-Publication Data

Dicker, Katie.
  You can draw exotic pets! / Katie Dicker.
      pages cm. — (Draw your pet!)
  Includes index.
  ISBN 978-1-4339-8736-6 (pbk.)
  ISBN 978-1-4339-8737-3 (6-pack)
  ISBN 978-1-4339-8735-9 (library binding)
  1. Animals in art—Juvenile literature. 2. Exotic animals—Juvenile literature. 3. Drawing—Technique—Juvenile literature. I. Title.
  NC783.8.P48D53 2013
  743.6—dc23

                                    2012033134

Published in 2013 by
Gareth Stevens Publishing
111 East 14th Street, Suite 349
New York, NY 10003

© 2013 Gareth Stevens Publishing

Produced for Gareth Stevens by Calcium Creative Ltd
Illustrated by Mike Lacey
Designed by Paul Myerscough
Edited by Sarah Eason and Harriet McGregor

Photo credits: Shutterstock: Sascha Burkard 14b, 16, Cynoclub 24, Irina Oxilixo Danilova 10t, Sebastian Duda 6t, Karel Gallas 22t, Tim Harman 18t, Infografick cover, 6b, Eric Isselée 8, Jagodka 10b, Masaki Norton 26t, Smit 22b, Tony Wear 18b, 20, Worldswildlifewonders 4, 14t, Pan Xunbin 26b, 28, Steshkin Yevgeniy 12.

Printed in the United States of America

CPSIA compliance information: Batch CW13GS: For further information contact Gareth Stevens, New York, New York at 1-800-542-2595.

Contents

You Can Draw Exotic Pets!

If you love exotic pets, you'll love to draw them, too! You can keep all kinds of animals as pets, from chameleons and tree frogs to chinchillas and even fiddler crabs!

Exotic pets are unlike more common pets, such as cats, birds, and dogs. Exotic creatures have much more unusual needs, so it is important to learn as much as you can about an exotic animal before you choose it as a pet. In this book, we'll teach you how to care for different types of exotic animals—and how to draw them, too.

Discover how to draw exotic pets!

Follow the steps on each page that show you how to draw each type of exotic animal. Then try using photographs of your own pet to create a special pet portrait!

You Will Need:

- Art paper and pencils
- Eraser
- Coloring pens and/or paints and a paintbrush

fiddler crabs

chinchillas

chameleons

tree frogs

opossums

tortoises

Chameleons

Chameleons are lizards that can change their color to blend in with their environment. These amazing creatures have huge eyes that swivel to see in every direction. Chamelons also have a long, curling tail.

Chameleons come in lots of colors from pink, blue, red, and orange to turquoise, yellow, and green.

Step 1

Draw the shape of the chameleon. Be sure to include both the branch and the lizard's curling tail. Pencil the jagged spines on the back.

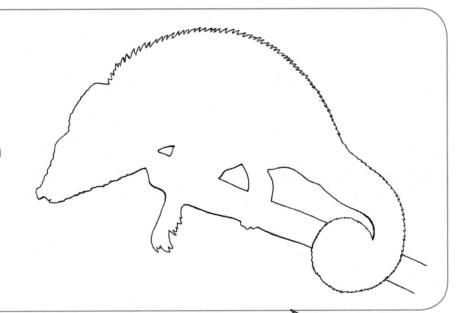

Step 2

Go over the outline with a thicker pencil. Then carefully draw the lizard's legs and the curling tip of its tail.

Step 3

Now add the lizard's eye and the scaly pattern along its jaw. Then add the ridge on the lizard's head.

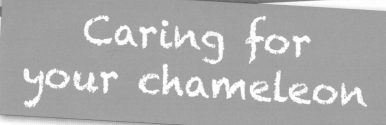

Caring for your chameleon

- Unlike cats and dogs, chameleons do not like to be petted and handled very often. Try to enjoy your pet just by watching it!

- Chameleons love to eat insects. Feed your pet grasshoppers, worms, and other insects you can buy from exotic pet stores.

- Buy an enclosure for your chameleon from an exotic pet store. Chameleons need to live in very warm environments, so the enclosure must be heated at all times to keep your lizard happy.

Chameleons live in hot places such as Africa, Asia, Spain, and Portugal.

Step

Now begin to add detail to your drawing. Carefully draw the scaly pattern on the chameleon's body. Add the detail on the lizard's eye and some light shading.

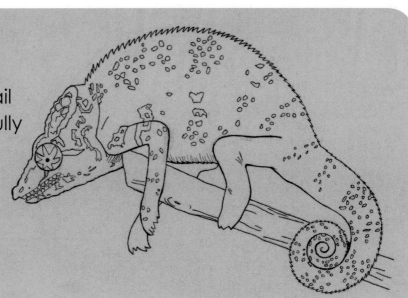

Step 5

Complete your chameleon by coloring it. Use shades of green for the body and add yellow and brown markings. For the head and eye, use yellow and add the brown markings. Color the branch brown. Finally, add highlights.

Chinchillas

The chinchilla is a cute-looking rodent with big ears, a long tail, and lots of soft, fluffy fur. These adorable pets are nocturnal, which means they sleep in the day and are active at night. Chinchillas can become very tame and loving with their owners.

Chinchillas have more fur per square inch than any other animal!

Step 1

Draw the outline of your chinchilla. Include the pet's large right ear and the soft, fluffy fur on the tail.

Step 2

Now draw the left ear and the tip of the paws at the front of the chinchilla. Carefully pencil the folds on the ears.

Step 3

Draw the animal's large, round eyes and the markings above them. Pencil the nose and the shape of the mouth and belly.

Caring for your chinchilla

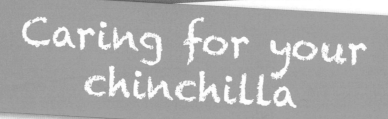

- Chinchillas need to live in cool temperatures, so be sure your pet does not become too hot.

- Give your chinchilla lots of toys such as balls and squeaky animals—it will love to play with them.

- Make sure you buy a large enclosure for your pet. Curious chinchillas need plenty of space to move around when they are awake at night.

Baby chinchillas are called "kits."

Step 4

Add lots of short pencil strokes for the animal's fur. Shade the eyes with a thick-tipped pencil.

Step 5

Now color the chinchilla. Use a mixture of light and dark gray for the fur. Leave areas on the chest, hind leg, and around the eyes white for highlights. Color the ears pink.

Tree Frogs

They may seem like a strange pet, but lots of people love to keep frogs as pets. The tree frog is an amazing creature. Its feet have very long toes with large sticky pads. The sticky pads help the tree frog to grip on to branches as it climbs up tall trees.

The red-eyed tree frog lives in rain forests such as the Amazon.

Step 1

Draw the shape of the frog. Carefully pencil the rounded outline of the eyes and the lines of the padded feet.

Step 2

Now add the frog's legs. Keep a steady hand, and slowly draw the shapes. Then add the outline of the frog's rounded belly.

Step 3

Now you can begin to add detail. Carefully shade the rim of the right eye, then add the pupil. Draw the lines on the left eye. Add the nostril and line of the mouth.

Caring for your tree frog

- Small- and medium-sized tree frogs eat insects. Larger tree frogs will make a meal of a small mammal and will even eat small lizards!

- Buy a large glass enclosure for your pet from an exotic pet store. Most tree frogs need a wet environment, so you will need a humidifier to keep your pet moist.

- Line the bottom of your enclosure with crushed coconut bark or peat moss. Add small tree branches so your pet can do what it does best—climb!

Tree frogs are often colored to match their surroundings. This helps them to hide from any predators.

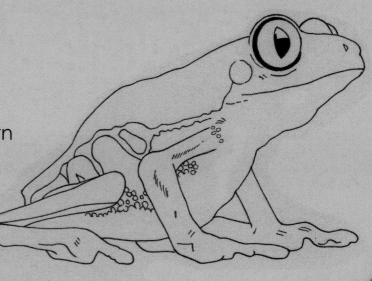

Now add the detailed markings on the body. Draw the speckled pattern and the larger markings on the belly. Add some lines around the frog's right eye.

Step 5

Color the back and legs of the tree frog with a bright lime-green color. Use a rich blue for the markings on the belly and a shade of brown for the other markings on the belly and neck. Use a rich orange-brown color for the feet. Finally, paint the eyes bright red and add white highlights.

Opossums

The opossum is an adorable-looking animal that makes a cute pet. It is around the size of a large rat and has gray fur. Opossums have five toes on each foot and a long tail that is completely bald!

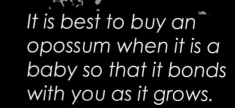

It is best to buy an opossum when it is a baby so that it bonds with you as it grows.

Step

Begin your drawing by penciling the opossum's head and ear. Then add the body, feet, and the tail.

Step

Draw the toes on the feet and the ears on the animal's head. Use a fine-tipped pencil for this stage.

Step

Now add detail by drawing the long, slanted eyes. Add the fur on the neck, head, and top of the legs.

Caring for your opossum

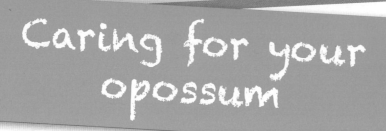

- Feed your opossum fruit and vegetables. Opossums also love eggs and cashew nuts.

- It is best to keep just one opossum as a pet. Two opossums are likely to fight each other.

- Opossums are always active at night. To get a good night's sleep, make sure you keep your pet's enclosure away from any bedrooms!

Opossums use their thick tail as a fifth "leg" for holding on to branches as they climb.

Step 4

Cover your cute opossum in fur by drawing hundreds of short, fine pencil strokes. Shade the eyes, leaving two white highlights.

Step 5

Color the opossum with a palette of grays and a very soft, light brown. Use a very light blue pencil for the top hairs on the fur. Leave the tip of the right ear and the center and cheeks of the face white.

Tortoises

A tortoise can live for between 50 and 100 years, so if you want to keep one as a pet, it will need to be a pet for life! Tortoises are one of the world's oldest animals—they have lived on Earth for thousands of years.

If frightened, a tortoise will pull its legs and head inside its thick shell to protect itself.

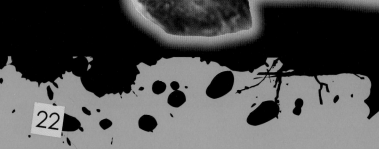

Step 1

Draw the outline of the tortoise, taking care to arch the neck. Include the tail and the claws on the front foot.

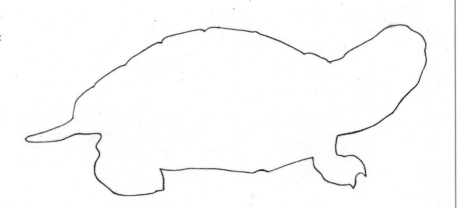

Step 2

Now add the outline of the tortoise's shell and the shape of its short, thick legs.

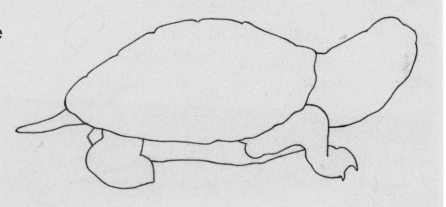

Step 3

Pencil the claw markings on the feet. Then add the tortoise's large, round eye and the folds on its neck and head.

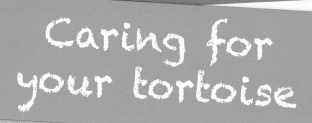

Caring for your tortoise

- You should only think about keeping a tortoise as a pet if you have a backyard. These animals need plenty of space to roam in.

- Keep your tortoise in a hutch with a run. You can buy one from most pet stores. If you let your tortoise roam free at times, be sure to watch it. Otherwise it might escape from your backyard and wander off!

- If you live in a place that has cold weather, you may need to bring your tortoise indoors. Tortoises don't like the cold and are better suited to warmer weather.

Tortoises love to eat fresh vegetables such as lettuce.

Step 4

Add the pattern on the tortoise's shell. Draw the outline of the tiles, then draw the pattern within them. Add the markings on the neck and face, then shade the eyes.

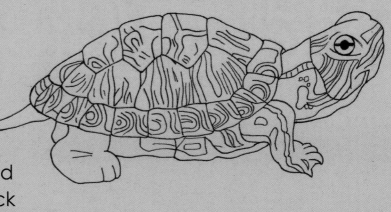

Step 5

Use shades of green for the shell, tail, neck, and the legs. Add shading to the rear leg, belly, and neck with a gray pencil. Carefully paint the markings on the face with a light green color. Finally, color the eye with a light blue shade.

Fiddler Crabs

Fiddler crabs live in shallow water near the shore. When the tide goes out, the crabs hide in rock pools or pockets of water left behind on the beach. These crabs are scavengers and feed on whatever they can find.

Male fiddler crabs have one large claw. Females have two claws.

Step 1

Draw the outline of the crab, taking care to pencil the eye stalks and the crab's dainty legs.

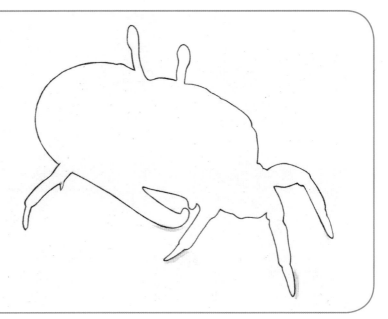

Step 2

Now add the large, powerful claw and the raised front leg.

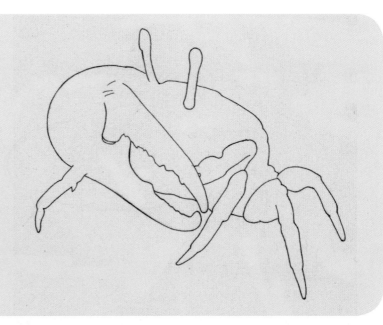

Step 3

Pencil the markings on the eyes and add light shading marks to the legs and head.

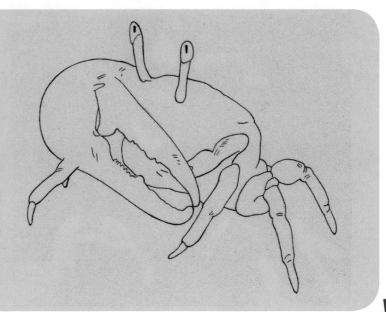

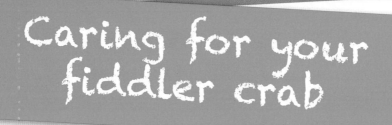

- Keep your crab in a tank that has an area of water, but also an area of dry rock and sand. Fiddler crabs like to spend time on dry land as much as they love to be in the water.

- Put some aquatic salt in your tank—this will make the water more like the sea, which is better for your fiddler crab.

- Don't be surprised if your fiddler crab sheds its shell! The outer layer of the shell is called an exoskeleton and when the crab molts, it shakes it off.

Fiddler crabs grow to around 2 inches (5 cm) across their body.

Step 4

Draw more shading marks, then add the lines on the claw and the pattern on the fiddler crab's back.

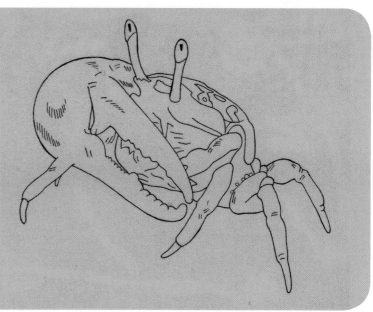

Step 5

Color the huge claw with a crimson red. Use shades of red for the legs. Use a deep brown-black color for the body. Then add light green-gray markings on the top of the back. Color the eyes with a light gray. Finally, add white highlights to the eyes, large claw, and legs.

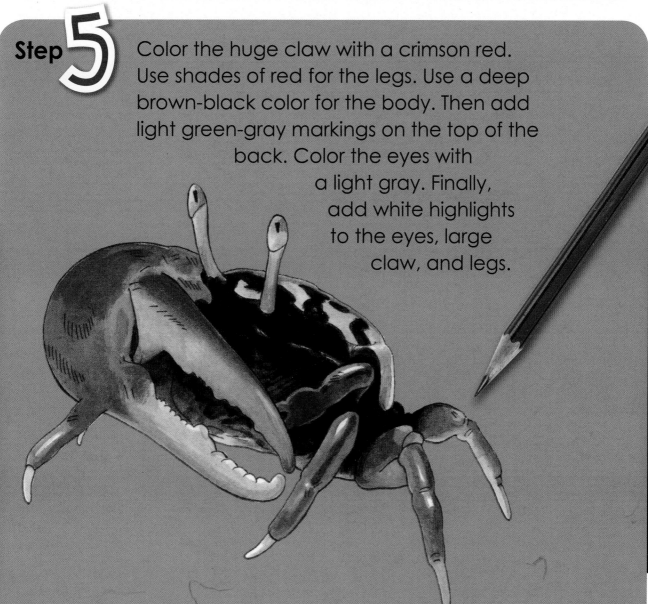

Glossary

active: moving

aquatic salt: a type of salt that is suitable for fish tanks

bark: the hard outer layer of a tree

bond: to become attached to an animal or a person

curious: wanting to find out about things

detail: the fine pencil markings on a drawing

enclosure: a container or an area in which an animal can be kept

environment: an area in which something lives

exoskeleton: the outer, hard structure of an insect or crustacean, such as a crab

exotic: not commonly found, unusual

humidifier: a device that sprays water or steam

lizard: a cold-blooded creature with a scaly skin

markings: the patterns on an animal's fur, feathers, or scales

molt: to shed fur or skin

nostril: the opening through which something breathes

palette: a range of colors

peat moss: a spongy plant that grows in very wet places

pet: stroke or cuddle

predator: creature that hunts and eats other creatures

rain forest: large forest in which a lot of rain falls

roam: to wander around

rodent: an animal with a furry body, long tail, and sharp front teeth. Rats and mice are types of rodent.

scavenger: creature that feeds on the remains of another animal's food or on dead and decaying remains

shade: to add depth to a picture with heavy pencil strokes

For More Information

Books

Barnes, Julia. *101 Facts About Exotic Pets*. Lydney, UK: Ringpress, 2002.

Cuddy, Robbin. *Learn to Draw Rainforest and Jungle Animals*. Irvine, CA: Walter Foster, 2013.

Levin, Freddie. *1-2-3 Draw Wild Animals*. Cincinnati, OH: Peel Productions, 2001.

Soloff Levy, Barbara. *How to Draw Wild Animals*. Mineoloa, NY: Dover Publications, 1999.

Websites

Find out more about all kinds of unusual animals at:
www.kidsbiology.com/animals-for-children.php

Discover more about exotic pets at:
www.petsclan.com/top-5-exotic-pets-kids.html

Index